Milet Publishing
Smallfields Cottage, Cox Green
Rudgwick, Horsham, West Sussex
RH12 3DE England
info@milet.com
www.milet.com
www.milet.co.uk

First English–French edition published by Milet Publishing in 2013

Copyright © Milet Publishing, 2013

ISBN 978 1 84059 824 7

Original Turkish text written by Erdem Seçmen
Translated to English by Alvin Parmar and adapted by Milet

Illustrated by Chris Dittopoulos
Designed by Christangelos Seferiadis

Printed and bound in Turkey by Ertem Matbaası

My Bilingual Book

Taste
Le goût

English–French

Close your eyes, taste this drink . . .

Ferme les yeux, goûte cette boisson . . .

Water or soda, what do you think?

À ton avis, est-ce de l'eau ou du soda ?

How do you know which one it is?

Comment le sais-tu ?

Do your mouth and tongue feel a fizz?

Ta bouche et ta langue sentent-elles des bulles ?

Your mouth and tongue let you taste drinks and food.

Ta bouche et ta langue te permettent de goûter les boissons et les aliments

They tell you what tastes bad and what tastes good!

Elles te disent ce qui a bon et mauvais goût !

Your taste senses bitter, sour, sweet,

Le goût te dit si c'est amer, aigre, doux

and salty, like the crackers you eat.

ou salé, comme les crackers que tu manges.

Some like the taste of chocolate best.

Certains préfèrent le goût du chocolat.

Most like the taste of medicine less!

Peu aiment le goût des médicaments !

It's fun to think about yummy sweets,

Tu adores les délicieux bonbons,

but eating too many is bad for your teeth!

mais en manger trop n'est pas bon pour tes dents !

Foods like peppers can be so hot!

Certains aliments comme le piment sont épicés !

Your taste will tell you to eat them or not.

Ton goût te dira si tu dois les manger.

Some tastes go together and some really don't mix,

Certains goûts se marient bien et d'autres pas,

like that banana and cheese sandwich you are about to fix!

comme cette banane et ce sandwich au fromage que tu prépares !

These delicious fruits deserve a nibble.

Ces délicieux fruits méritent d'être grignotés.

They're good for your body and irresistible!

Ils sont irrésistibles et bons pour la santé !

Trying different foods makes your taste sense grow.

Plus tu manges d'aliments différents, plus ton sens du goût se développ

Your world gets bigger, the more foods that you know!

Plus tu connais d'aliments, plus ton univers grandit !